Thomas Goldney's Garden

The creation of an eighteenth century garden

P. K. Stembridge

First published by Avon Gardens Trust
to mark the tercentenary in July 1996
of the birth of Thomas Goldney,
creator of Goldney garden, Clifton

ISBN 0 9518290 2 5

Printed by Burleigh Press Limited, Bristol BS2 0YA

'And each congenial guest with joy invades
The fountains, grottos, and the clear cascades; . . .
A minor Stow on Clifton's crown we find,
In Epic meekness, like its master's mind.'

Henry Jones: 'Clifton' 1766

Goldney garden in Clifton, Bristol, has been an attraction for visitors since its creation in the eighteenth century. The garden we see today has been altered to some extent in area and design over the years and it has of course evolved by growth and decay. Today's visitor can see almost all of the important structural features from the 1760s: the orangery at the head of the canal, the tower and rotunda at either end of the great terrace, the bastion in the paddock below. The famous and unique central feature – the grotto – is still approached at the end of the main axis from the house through an avenue of yew trees, with the statue of Hercules in place on the terrace above the grotto entrance. Although the prospects outward from the garden are materially altered, the viewing points remain. The garden was chiefly the vision of one man: Thomas Goldney, a Quaker merchant. He was the third generation with the same name of a family established in Bristol in the seventeenth century. His grandfather, Thomas I, had come to Bristol as an apprentice grocer in 1637 and nine years later he became a burgess or freeman able to follow his trade in the city. In the 1650s Thomas I and his wife Mary joined the new movement of the Society of Friends or Quakers and became active members of the group. Their son, Thomas II, born in 1664, gained the freedom of the city in his turn in 1688. He married the daughter of Thomas Speed, a prosperous Quaker merchant, but was less active in the Quaker movement than his parents and father-in-law had been. Like them, he was enterprising and successful, and well respected by his fellow citizens. In 1694, it was Thomas II who made the move from a merchant's house in High Street in the heart of the city to a gentleman's house in Clifton.

The house at the top of Clifton hill, opposite the church, had belonged to Lord Folliot, an Irish peer, who had given it in 1692 as part of his daughter's marriage settlement, but her new husband already had an estate in Shropshire. So Thomas Goldney II was able to rent the house with its garden and orchard in 1694, and to move there with his wife Martha and three surviving children. In July 1696, their sixth child, a son – Thomas III – was born in the Clifton house, followed in the next eleven years by six more children, of whom two sons and three daughters survived childhood. Then, for nearly a century, the house was the home for members of these two generations of the Goldney family.

Described as a mansion, the house fronted the road coming up the hill from the city and leading on towards the Downs. The garden, a rectangular plot of some two acres in extent, lay mostly behind and to the south of the house. It already had something of the character of a gentleman's garden, as there was a special mention in the original lease of 'statues, figures and flower pots', which were to be preserved by the tenant 'in as good condition as the same now are'. In 1705, Thomas Goldney took up his option to buy the house and continued to care for and improve the garden. He employed a gardener and his apprentice, and from time to time a 'weeder woman' at sixpence a day. When he had spare capital from the profits that were realised in 1712 and 1713 on his investment in Captain Woodes Rogers's eminently successful privateering voyage of the *Duke* and the *Dutchess,* he had a large 'greenhouse' built. This was begun in 1714, and Goldney paid local workmen, including a glazier and a tiler, for a fairly extensive structure. These newly popular buildings were intended for the over-wintering of tender evergreens and for growing citrus fruits. It is this latter use which has given the name orangery to the handsome garden buildings. The greenhouse was not in the same position as the present orangery, but according to the map of 1746 was about halfway along the then western edge of the garden. [see map p. 13]

In the 1720s Thomas Goldney II not only set about rebuilding the Clifton house, but he made a number of further additions and improvements to the grounds and garden features. He bought gates and a quantity of pallisades from the iron works at Coalbrookdale in Shropshire, founded by Abraham Darby, in which Goldney had a major financial share and which was his main business interest after 1717. Later, the railings were in place as part of the southern boundary of Goldney's garden, and this suggests that Thomas Goldney II had contrived a viewing point to look outward from his garden, as recommended by the landscape writers of the time. In 1725 he employed a local craftsman, Francis Billo, on 'figures and work about his fountain'. Two years later he bought a large quantity of 'French grass seed' and so must have been either making or re-seeding lawns or grass walks. When Thomas Goldney II died in 1731, the garden and newly built house were inherited by his son, Thomas III. Although there is unfortunately no further evidence of what the garden was like at this time, it was obviously well-cared for, with some interesting and important features.

At the time of his father's death, Thomas III was a 35-year-old bachelor, probably living in one of the four houses owned by the family at Castle

Green in the city. He had originally begun his adult working life as cashier and clerk at Coalbrookdale after the death of Abraham Darby in 1717. Six years later Thomas returned to Bristol to join his father as the Coalbrookdale or Dale Company's agent and 'banker' in Bristol. The work involved receiving shipments of goods arriving at the docks by trow from Coalbrookdale, checking cargoes at the quayside, dealing with the trowmen, arranging for the warehousing, sale or re-shipment of the various kinds of iron ware, collecting payment, keeping accounts, and making occasional visits to the works in Shropshire. For his work as cashier and company representative Thomas III had received a salary of £50 a year and he owned two shares, 1/8 of the Dale Company stock, on which dividends were paid. With his new inheritance, which included the family coach and horses, he was comfortably off. However, although the family had clearly moved up the social scale and Thomas Goldney III was soon interested in enlarging the Clifton estate, he showed no inclination to give up his business interests. In fact, he expanded and diversified them over the next 30 years with considerable financial success. The returns from these business ventures – additional ironworks connected with Coalbrookdale, a share in the Champion copper and brass works at Warmley, investment in mining in Flintshire, shares in three small ships, partnership in a new bank in Bristol – provided the money to enable him to extend his estate and develop his chief leisure interest: the creation of an unusual garden.

It is possible to trace Goldney's plans about the piecemeal building up of the estate from the sequence of deeds that have survived, but it is more difficult to deduce his ideas about the design and creation of the garden. Unfortunately, if there ever were definite plans or precise notes they have not survived. It is also impossible to say what exactly were his models and inspiration. Generally, there was considerable interest in garden-making and design among the well-to-do in the early eighteenth century, encouraged

3

by the writings of Addison, Pope, Switzer and others. From aristocratic and literary beginnings, ideas were filtering through to those with smaller scope in land and finance. From the beginnings of Quakerism in the mid-seventeenth century too, Friends who were 'cut off by their precepts from so many of the recreations of life' took a great interest in their gardens and were encouraged to do so by Quaker leaders, such as William Penn. A garden provided a peaceful retreat and 'a healthy means of escape from public and social life'. Several of the now famous eighteenth century botanists and plantsmen were Quakers, some of whom were known to Goldney, particularly the Collinsons of Mill Hill. Increasing numbers of books of advice on gardens and gardening were being published from the 1720s onwards, and the Gentleman's Magazine, which began publishing in 1731, carried articles on practical gardening. For Thomas Goldney, it may also have happened, as with many people today, that ownership of a piece of land was sufficient stimulus to gardening activities, though not everyone is able to create something as remarkable and of such lasting interest as Goldney did.

He did not, however, begin on innovations at once, as he was much occupied with the additional responsibilities and new projects at Coalbrookdale. At midsummer 1732 he appointed a new gardener, Adam Sixsmith, who proved hard-working and trustworthy, and who was to remain in charge for over 36 years. The garden was first extended in 1733 by the purchase of a paddock of one and a half acres adjoining the original eastern boundary. This area seems to have become the kitchen garden and an orchard with some of the fruit trees trained against the eastern wall, which was the boundary with the road leading from the church down towards Jacob's Well [now Constitution Hill]. A brief description of the garden four years after Thomas III inherited it is given by a visitor to Bristol in the early summer of 1735. John Kelsall, a Quaker formerly associated with Abraham Darby at Coalbrookdale and certainly acquainted with both the Goldneys, father and son, recorded in his journal for 3 June 1735 that he walked up from the Hotwell

> 'to Thos. Goldneys at Clifton, went thro his Gardens &c which are very fine with Walks, Greens, Waterworks, Summer Houses &c there were many Lemons and Orange Trees with fruit on them'.

The 'Greens' were evergreens and the last comment suggests that the greenhouse was in good working order. The year after Kelsall's visit, late in 1736, Goldney began to use a small home-made notebook, which he labelled 'Garden Book', to record work in the garden, and this suggests the real beginning of his interest as a gardener.

Entries in the note book in the first year, before any of the major works in the garden were begun, show what some of these interests were in planting, sowing and grafting. Goldney was extending an existing 'Filbeard Grove' [*Corylus maxima*] and planting more nut trees at the southern end of the new paddock. He refers to a new holly hedge, and there was also an established elm hedge or walk as well as gravel walks and a Long Walk with box edgings. Goldney sowed sunflower seed in May and white and purple broccoli seed in June. He put notched sticks by anemones indicating their colours and which were the best. An important interest was the budding or grafting of fruit trees; pears were mentioned in this first year's records and in later years apples and other tree fruits were grafted in the spring or budded in the summer. He had some new tubs made, and one of his China Orange trees and some aloes were transplanted into them. He also evidently had some vines near the house, but after he had begun his first major garden project and bought additional land, he was able to plant a small vineyard, though he continued to have vines within his main garden.

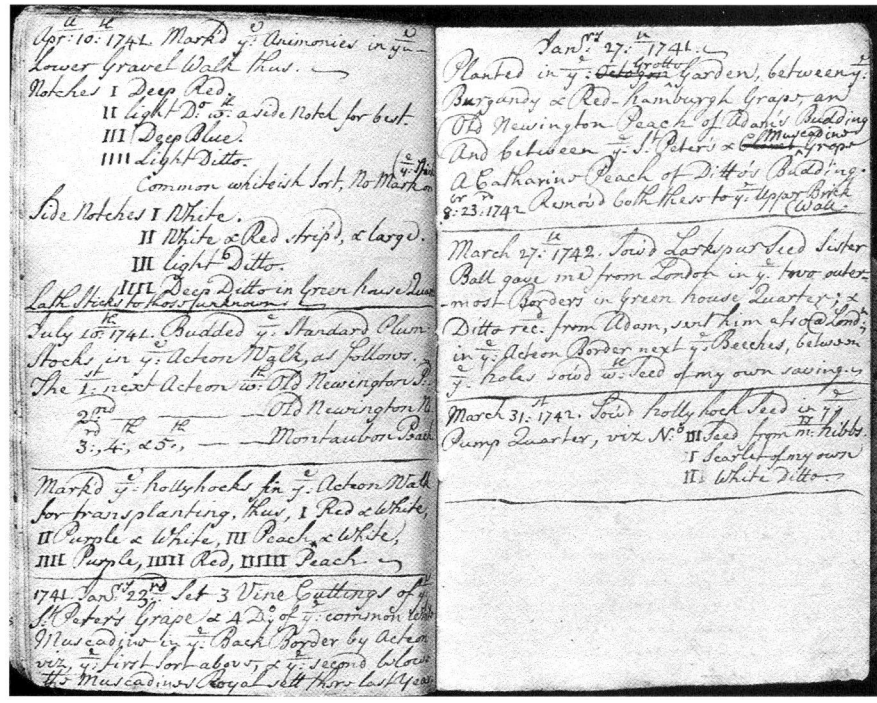

Pages from Thomas Goldney's Garden Book.

Grotto

In the summer of 1737, Goldney began on the first important and central part of his garden scheme, the construction of a grotto. It is only possible to speculate on the inspiration for Goldney's plans for his garden as there is no surviving evidence of particular gardens that he knew from which he took ideas for his own, and as a grotto-builder he was something of an innovator. He would have heard his father's account of interesting gardens visited during his tour of the Netherlands in 1725 and perhaps been intrigued by a description of the 'most curiouse Grotto in Shell-Work, very admirable Workmanship' in the garden of a rich merchant near Utrecht, with 'variety of Fancys as if twas in paint, & all this compos:d by assortment of Shells in colour & shape to answer ye designe of ye compiler'. In England, although Alexander Pope was developing his garden and grotto at Twickenham in the 1720s, and liked to give advice on gardens to his friends, the Catholic poet and the Quaker business man were not even acquainted and did not have the same circle of friends. Goldney did not employ a professional garden designer, but like many other enthusiastic amateurs worked out his own plans over a period of time.

Goldney's scheme was ambitious and depended for completion on his being able to buy additional land on his southern boundary. Two plots there belonging to individual owners were evidently not immediately available, and he had to be content at first with one slightly to the south west which was not adjacent to his own garden. When he bought this plot from his neighbour, Robert Smith, in July 1737, a clause was specifically included in the contract to give Goldney liberty

> 'to make a Subterranious passage or Footway under Ground of commodious dimensions (not exceeding Eight Foot Wide & Eight Foot high in the clear when walled and arched over) from the said TG's garden to the said piece of ground'.

The document is labelled in Goldney's writing 'land for the grotto garden'. The position of this plot and perhaps the intervening public footpath would account for the line of the tunnel, and provides some resemblance to Pope's garden where the two parts separated by the Hampton road were linked by a grotto tunnel. The work was evidently begun promptly and carried out expeditiously, as Goldney noted

> 'Finish'd the subterraneous Passage to the Grotto Anno 1737 — And began upon the Grotto the same Year', though the whole complex and fantastically decorated structure was not completed for another 27 years. [See R.J.G. Savage: *Natural History of the Goldney Garden Grotto* for a definitive survey of the layout, design and decoration.] The same deed of 1737 also

included the restriction that Robert Smith was not to obstruct

'the view of a Walk ... leading southward from the Freestone front of the said TG's house to an iron pallisade at the S. end of the said Walk'.

This pallisade is probably the one bought from Coalbrookdale in the spring of 1723. It appears as a row of nine spear-headed palings on a sketch plan made by Goldney in June 1747. The Long Walk to the viewpoint was grass, bordered with evergreens and with box edgings. It was the main avenue in the garden, and was later to lead to steps down to the door of the grotto.

A year after the tunnel was finished, and while the main grotto-building was in progress, in January 1739, Goldney bought two more pieces of land in the vicinity, from his neighbour, Robert Smith. One was Hill Close, a meadow of some six acres, adjoining Goldney's western boundary, and the other was a smaller paddock of two and a half acres to the south of the Close, adjoining both his own garden and the small plot he had already acquired. In the new grotto garden which was entered from the archway at the southern end of the tunnel, Goldney immediately planted beeches on a terrace walk and also put in a row of named varieties of vines.

Work on the construction of the grotto continued so well, that Goldney could record 'cover'd and finish'd ye shell of ye Grotto Aug. 1739', and this is confirmed by the date and his initials in a pattern of shells – 17 TG 39 – under the skylight nearest to the doorway to the tunnel. By September 1749, when the Revd Alexander Catcott, vicar of Temple church in Bristol, visited the garden, a good deal more was completed and Goldney evidently spoke of his plans for the next stages. According to Catcott, the grotto

'consists of 3 rooms, parted by pillars, that on the left hand finished with regard to the Shell-work'.

The shells at this end of the grotto are most elaborately arranged to produce three-dimensional effects. The four pillars are completely decorated with Bristol Stones or 'diamonds', clusters of small quartz crystals. In an earlier entry in his Journal, Catcott had commented that these Stones

'are not to be found now in the Plenty they were formerly, for Mr Goldney of Clifton has employed men for 7 last years on purpose to gather them, to adorn his Grotto'.

This is probably an exaggeration, though the quantity of the Bristol diamonds used is amazing. The small pool which was to receive the water falling 'from out of an urn of a Sea-God, seated (reclined on his Elbow) ... on a rising ground' was not yet completed, but 'A Gloomy den in which there is to be a lion' was ready opposite the entrance door, though 'the Lion [is] not yet made'.

The next visitor to leave an account of the grotto after a visit in November 1756 was Mrs Delany. Although she said it was 'not much more than half finished' she thought it 'one of the few things that answers expectation'. The pool had been constructed and she saw the cascade flowing into it. She also mentioned the 'sort of rocky cave' but the lions were evidently not yet in residence. The following year the front of the grotto 'all save the Freestone Window Frames' was finished and from 1757 to 1759, Goldney employed John Warwell at considerable expense to add the decorative rock and shell work round the pool.

Work then seems to have continued more speedily, and by the time of the visit by the Duchess of Northumberland in the early 1760s, the grotto was complete and much of the floor had been laid. She described this as a 'Pavement of Tiles glaz'd wch nearly resemble Egyptian Pebbles'. The tiles are very attractive small quarries, made of glazed and fired clays. As Professor Savage points out, these are unusual as grotto flooring in the eighteenth century, another instance of the individuality of Goldney's design. The plain and patterned tiles in brownish-red, yellow and black were bought from the Coalbrookdale brick and tile works; although expensive, they were not the costliest item in the grotto. From February 1762 to March 1765 Thomas Paty, the skilled Bristol stonemason, was paid for 'grinding, gageing & laying' the tiles.

The lion and lioness must have been in their cave by this time, but the Duchess only mentions 'a Lyon carv'd in Stone as large as the Life' at one end of the terrace, where he still lies. Later visitors commented on the effect of terror produced by the lions in their den, another of Goldney's unusual ideas for his grotto; it conformed to Burke's concept of 'delightful horror', fear within the realm of pleasure, though not in the landscape, but in the confines of an underground grotto. The lion in front of the cave is made of plaster and the pair may well have been painted, which would have made them look more lifelike, especially in dim light. It is strange that the Duchess does not mention them as she was obviously very much impressed by all she saw in the garden and in 'this most magnificent Grotto'. Although she found it

> 'impossible to describe the Variety there is of Shells Fossils Oars Sparres Petrifactions &c &c to adorn this place most of wch were placed here by the hand of Mr Gouldney himself',

she left one of the most comprehensive accounts, including this vivid description:

'at one End of the Grotto sitts a River God who from an Urn throws a clear Stream wch trickles over the Shells &c in a wild Cascade into a Bason . . . on each Side of this Cascade is a large rough kind of Scollop the inside Mother of Pearl wch came from the E Indies.'

It is just possible that these giant clams had been brought back 40 years before by Captain Woodes Rogers and presented to the family of his patron. Thomas Goldney must have found the Duchess a very satisfactory visitor, so appreciative of his work, though the design for the whole garden was not quite completed. The tower and the Fire-engine were yet to come.

Bastion

At an early stage of Goldney's development of his garden, there are intriguing references in his Garden Book to two of the architectural features with unexplained origins: the bastion and the rotunda. Neither of these appears as such on the 1746 map, but Goldney's notes suggest that they must have been in existence in some form. It is possible that the rotunda and the rounded western end of the bastion may have developed from what are shown on the map as two circular structures and described in the accompanying Survey as fruit closets.

Goldney's first specific reference to the bastion or mock fortification occurs in the Garden Book in 1748, when he recorded setting 'Vine cuttings under the Bastion in Poultry Garden', but the date of its construction is uncertain. In 1739, when Goldney bought the plot of land on which it stands, there was no mention in the deed of either a bastion or fruit closets, but at some time Goldney had written on the outside of the document 'Fort Garden', a term which occurs nowhere else among the surviving papers. Although Goldney made a note about the date of the construction of most of his other garden works, he does not mention the building of the bastion. A nineteenth century document, reciting various leases, includes the words 'on the said ground Thomas Goldney erected a certain building which he called the Bastion', but gives no date. In 1739, the construction of the grotto was a major pre-occupation, but Goldney is recorded as having built a wall along the northern boundary of his new land purchase, and this could have been the beginning of the construction of the bastion.

This mock fortification extends westward on the lower ground below the rotunda. Buttressed walls in local stone form parapets to a wide walk along the top to the western end, which widens to an oval; round windows like gun ports are below in the side walls. In the eighteenth century there was a good view from the walk to the shipping on the river, and Goldney could have watched the trows bringing goods from Coalbrookdale or his own ships among all the traffic there. The thick walls enclose a long wide corridor, with arched entrances on the south-facing side; the westernmost archway leads to a high vaulted chamber with apsidal ends, under the look-out. The bastion has some resemblance to designs by John Vanbrugh, such as the 'fortifications' including a bastioned wall built at Castle Howard in 1725, and the bastions of the kitchen garden at Claremont in 1723, and these may have been the inspiration for Goldney's bastion. There had been a close business connection between Thomas Goldney II and Carleton Vanbrugh, a younger brother of the architect, in the first decade of the century, and it is possible that the Goldney family knew John Vanbrugh personally, as he had designed Kings Weston House four miles away across the Downs [1710-14]. In spite of its military name and appearance, the bastion had prosaic uses, as fruit store and poultry house, and vines and fruit trees were grown against its southern wall. In modern times too, in the 1960s, the paddock provided grazing and the bastion sheltered sheep or cattle from the University of Bristol Veterinary Department. Although a somewhat bizarre structure, it was not an artificial ruin, or illusionary façade, a complete sham, such as adorned some other eighteenth century gardens, and it reflects Goldney's interest in the useful as well as the unusual.

Rotunda

The rotunda now forms a satisfying link between the lower level of the bastion and the higher level of the terrace. From the terrace walk, which it closes at the western end, it appears as a single storey structure, surrounded by a low perimeter wall, and surmounted with a decorative crown-like battlement in brick and stone. A narrow flight of steps curves down from the terrace level on the southern side, ending by an arched entry into a circular vaulted room at the level of the bastion walk. Goldney's earliest reference to the rotunda occurs in February 1739, but this was not the building as it appears today. The origin of the Goldney rotunda may have been the fruit closet marked on the 1746 map or possibly a summer house. According to references in the estate deeds, summer houses seem to have been popular in Clifton gardens during the eighteenth century. The plots to the south of Goldney's garden both had summer houses; one was 'built over an underground kitchen' as early as 1729. Goldney eventually acquired the first of these plots in January 1748 and the second in May 1753. He paid heavily for this latter purchase, but it at last completed the area he wanted for his own garden. It became part of the open paddock to the south of his new terrace, which was built up 'in the rough' above the grotto by 1755. The same year, he bought a large number of specimen trees to plant along his new southern boundary.

Sketch by S.H. Grimm, 1788.

Two years later, Goldney noted: 'Finish'd the Rotunda with the Colonade round it Anno 1757'. This suggests that, once the terrace was completed, Goldney turned his attention to rebuilding the rotunda or making it more decorative to close the vista at the western end by adding the 'colonade', slender columns resting on plinths in the parapet wall, and forming a covered walk. These can be seen in place in a sketch drawn by S. H. Grimm. The mixture of styles in the rotunda is referred to in a contemporary poem on Clifton as 'A Gothic building by a Greek embraced'. The colonnade seems to have been removed early in the nineteenth century. This alteration exposed walls which had been somewhat protected in a situation rather open to wind and rain and which then weathered badly; in 1969, they were restored with a light stone-coloured rendering. The door opening on to the terrace and the windows in each of the other sides have ogee-shaped heads with an attractive pattern of small panes. From the inside, three of the windows facing northwards have been blocked down to circular port-holes, 'yielding', according to Samuel Curwen, an American who visited the garden in 1776, 'three delightful perspectives'; from one of these – before any building development intervened – the handsome house belonging to Goldney's sister, Martha Champion, could be seen across Clifton Green. In Goldney's lifetime

11

the rotunda was furnished with 'a circular Virginia Walnut tree seat raised up' and four chairs of the same wood, evidently making a pleasant and interesting place to sit, with its near and distant views.

The Octagon or Pleasure house

Another summer house that was larger and even better furnished in Thomas Goldney's time has completely disappeared. In the 1760s the Duchess of Northumberland recorded seeing 'As soon as ye enter the Court before you come to ye House a Circular Summer [house] with Windows every way'. Called the Pleasure house or Octagon, it stood in the north-west corner of the garden, near Hill Close and the road. On Ashmead's map of 1828, an octagonal building is indicated in this situation, but it was taken down to allow for road widening a few years later. The only pictorial evidence is a small undated sketch. Like the rotunda, the Octagon had two storeys, but the inventory of 1768 shows that 'the Room under the Octagon' was evidently quite habitable. It was furnished with a table, chairs and writing desks and there was a fireplace, with bronze heads on brackets above it. The upper storey was even more comfortable, with 'Green Draw up Window Curtains', and a circular

Local Studies Library, Bristol Reference Library

Summer house in Mr Goldney's Garden

'painted canvas floor cloth', besides Windsor chairs and a mahogany table, and there were a number of pictures on the walls. Goldney frequently refers to the Pleasure house in his Garden Book, and it was probably one of the summer houses mentioned by Kelsall. It was well sited in the garden, allowing views in all directions. The view south from it was along one of the more important walks, perhaps punctuated by the statue of Acteon, on the way towards the original greenhouse by the west walk.

Section of map of the Manor of Clifton.

Goldney house and main garden are marked with Xs, and some of the additional plots with X . l and S.

Although the individual garden plans look rather stylised, some of the details are corroborated by other evidence; this suggests that de Wilstar had surveyed the area carefully. The Octagon, and the line of trees at the front of the house, for instance, are also shown on the map of 1828 [see inside back cover]; the building and trees were removed for road widening in the 1830s. The fruit closets, the footpath round two sides of the original garden, and presumably the greenhouse at the western edge of the garden are all shown.

View of Clifton from Rownham Meads, English school ca. 1785. This shows Goldney h⋯

Hyacinth:
King of
Great Britain.

Gardeners at w⋯
from painting⋯
Hartwell House⋯
Balthassar Nel⋯
ca. 1⋯

The Lindley Library,
Royal Horticultural Society
photograph: Ruth Duthie;

Buckinghams⋯
County Mus⋯

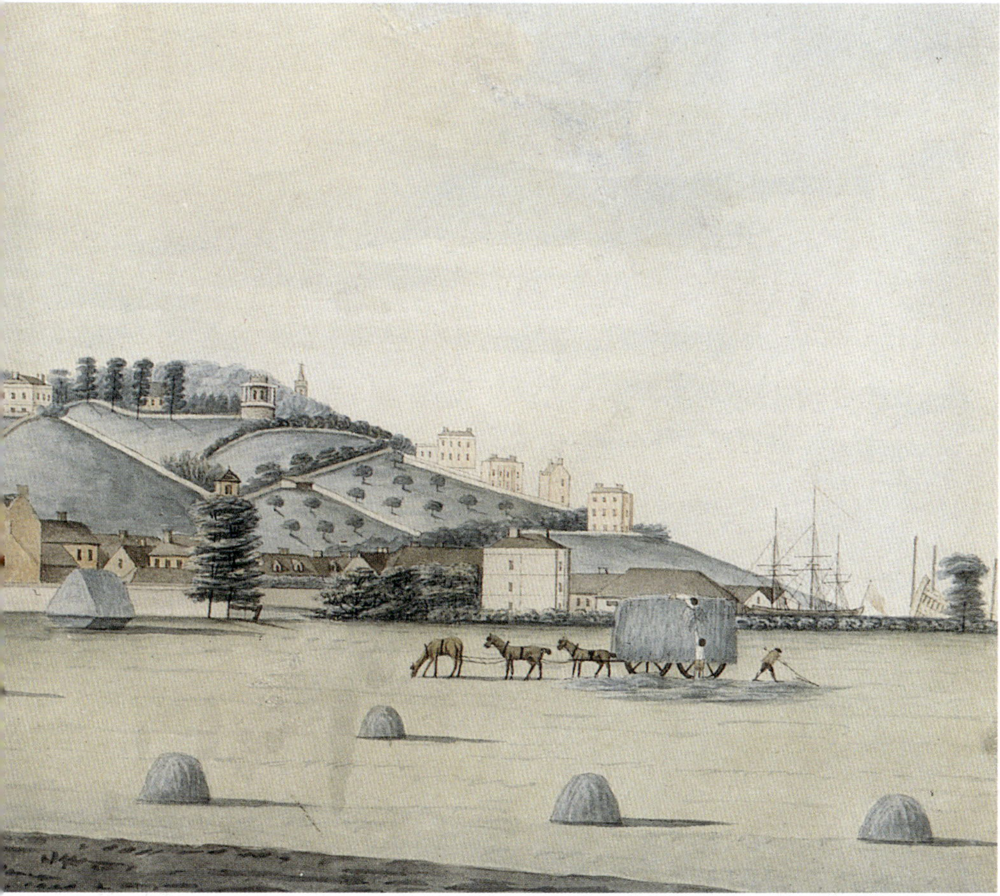

Octagon and the Rotunda on Clifton hill.

Bristol City Museum and Art Gallery

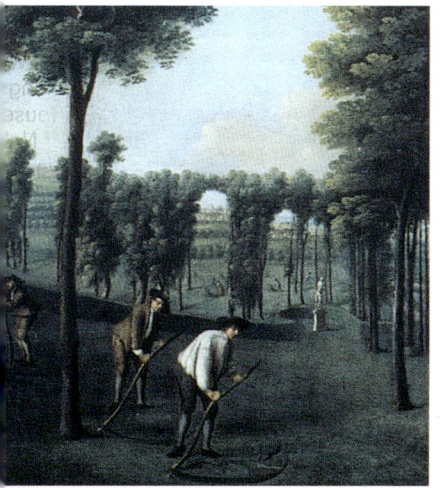

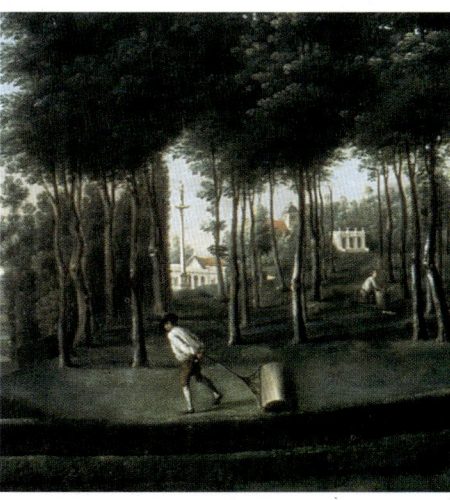

Cascade in Goldney grotto.

Arts Faculty Photographic Unit

Shells by the grotto pool.

The lions' cave.

Water features

There were evidently more extensive water features in Goldney's garden than have survived today. Thomas Goldney II had had 'work done about his fountain' in 1725 and Kelsall mentioned unspecified 'waterworks' in 1735. The only contemporary map, that of 1746, has no indication of pools, but the scale used was small, and the garden was represented in a fairly stylised way. In his Garden Book, Goldney refers to the 'Fountain garden' from 1739, twenty years before the canal was constructed. There are references to three ponds as well as the canal in 1768. One was 'by the fire Engine', that is, the tower, perhaps near the head of the well. The two others were 'before the Iron Gates' with figures of '2 Boys spouting Waters'. The gates seem to have been at the main entrance, from the road by Clifton church, and there were statues of Ceres and Bacchus near them, contributing to an entrance court suitable for a gentleman's residence.

There is more certain information about the canal, the 150-feet-long rectangle of water, now with an apsidal end, in the area south of the orangery. Goldney dated this as 'begun Anno 1758, & finish'd in the following year'. It would have been more logical and practical if the canal had been constructed before the terrace, and then the excavated earth could have been used to help build up the height required there. As the canal was constructed later, it was probably not in Goldney's earlier ideas for the design and layout of the garden. Instead, the 'mount' at the southern end of the canal was probably built up from the excavated soil. With its straight sides, the canal was not in the currently fashionable taste for the natural and serpentine, but was in the old-fashioned Dutch style of the end of the seventeenth century, like the formal water-garden with its canals and yew hedges at Westbury Court, a few miles away across the Severn. At Goldney, the situation and terrain of a flattish hill top were not really suitable for an irregular stretch of water, and there was no stream to be dammed and enlarged, even on the lower slopes in the paddock.

In Goldney's canal was a lead fountain, and a basin. Samuel Curwen noticed that this 'small piece of water [was] abounding in gold and silver fish'. Goldney had begun with a small collection of these before the canal was constructed, when he paid six shillings and sixpence 'for a Tub to bring Gold Fish in per Ship' from London. At the 'hither end' of the canal, nearer the orangery, were two lead statues, of Mercury and a Faun. At the other end, 'upon the mount at the head of the canal', were two more leaden figures of a man and a woman. This piece of rising ground between the southern end of the canal and the terrace was eventually 'made rough, scraggy, and woody, to resemble a wilderness', according to Curwen. The narrow, steep-sided, rock-lined path that winds through here to the kitchen garden produced a suitably 'Grotesque' effect in the damp shade of overhanging trees and shrubs, as it did until the recent tamer planting.

Tower and Fire-engine

There is unfortunately no evidence to show how the flow of water to the fountains and to the cascade in the grotto was originally powered, though the Duchess of Northumberland mentioned a windmill raising the water for the house and garden. When Curwen visited in 1776, he described the source of power for the fountain in the canal as a 'lofty fire-engine'. This is now more usually described as a beam engine, of the type invented by Newcomen early in the eighteenth century. The Coalbrookdale works had been producing the iron parts for these machines for many years when Goldney commissioned a small fire-engine for his own use in 1764. To house it, a tower was erected towards the eastern end of the terrace. Like the bastion, it was built of local stone, perhaps quarried from Goldney's own 'rocky ground' lower down in Clifton Wood. The basement of the tower, reached through a tunnel at the back of the grotto, housed the coal-fired boiler. There is a wide, walled trench beside the tower which would have been useful for storing the quantity of solid fuel required, out of sight of visitors to the garden. The unusual large arched opening on an upper floor of the tower was necessary to allow half of the engine beam to project to where the pipes went down to the well, some 130 feet deep. The head of this well is now underground, vaulted over with brick work, and accessible from the small tunnel to the left of the grotto entrance. On the inside of the tower wall are just discernible traces where the chimney must have been.

Unfortunately, it took some time to get the engine working satisfactorily. The first parts were shipped from the Dale in November and December 1764 but the cylinder proved too small. A second cylinder sent to replace it in the summer of 1766 was 15 inches in diameter and 9 feet 2 inches in length. Even this was very small in comparison with those being supplied to the Cornish mines, which were usually at least five feet in diameter. The boiler seems to have proved a problem too: Goldney noted that the first one sent was returned as too heavy and was exchanged for a lighter one, but a year later he received yet another boiler, this time with more holes bored. The new engine was eventually installed and working satisfactorily. Without its fire engine, the tower now resembles some other eighteenth century folly towers, but it had served a useful purpose. It is also unusual since most engine houses, like those at Coalbrookdale and in Cornwall, were square or rectangular, with external chimneys, but Goldney had some eye for the aesthetic and original as well as the functional. A French visitor in 1768 thought the Gothic tower 'très élégante' and commented on the Fire Engine supplying water to 'un grand bassin'. It seems to have been still in use in 1785, when it was mentioned by another visitor to the garden. As well as providing the power for the fountain in the canal, the engine pumped water from the well for the cascade in the grotto. An electric pump now supplies the power and recycles

Beighton's engraving of a Newcomen engine, 1717.

the water, but the effect is still exciting, as the water rushes down the narrow way, wearing channels in the rock, partly dispersing into the giant clam shells on either side, to flow in miniature waterfalls over their fluted rims into the deep pool surrounded by rock and shell work. Barbara Jones obviously thought it one of the best things she had seen in a grotto, and in *Follies and Grottoes* described it as 'theatrical and fine, a masterpiece of shifting light and water, sound and shadow'. The tower and the fire-engine were Goldney's last structural works in the garden and it is difficult to see what more he could have achieved.

Planting

While Thomas Goldney was obviously very dedicated to re-designing and creating a special garden he was also interested in practical gardening. He possessed copies of Switzer's *Practical Fruit Gardener,* published in 1724, and Miller's *Gardener's Dictionary,* which was first published in 1731. He also had copies of the *Gentleman's Magazine,* with its monthly gardening articles giving practical advice. Several of Goldney's notes suggest that such advice was not lost on him. When he moved some aloes and one of his China orange trees into new tubs, he noted the mixture of soil required for the aloes as 'half lime rubble and half light mould'. Some strawberry roots were 'set in holes fill'd with two measures of Hazell Mould & one of Melon Ditto'. Ranunculus roots were planted in a mixture 'three parts light mould to one part sand, eight inches apart and one inch deep, in a small trench'. One area of the garden was actually designated 'the Mould quarter', but it also contained some of Goldney's many fruit trees.

Yields of all crops were generally lower in the eighteenth century than today, and Goldney took some care in choosing and encouraging the 'good sorts'. In the summer of 1737, he was casting a critical eye over gooseberry bushes which had originally come from London, sorting those that were not worth saving from those that should be kept. The latter included 'large Chrystall, large Green and large Red'. The only other soft fruits mentioned beside the gooseberries and strawberries were red and white currants. These do not seem to have been confined to the kitchen garden, as it is clear that the quarters in the main garden contained very mixed planting: a good many fruit trees, some of which were espaliered, strawberries, currants and gooseberries, and presumably the vegetable after which the quarter was named: asparagus, artichoke or cucumber. Goldney comments less on the vegetables, and there is only one reference to broccoli seed being sown. Flowers seem to have been kept to the borders.

Fruit trees

Although Thomas Goldney does not seem to have been much interested in vegetable growing, which was perhaps considered the province of the gardeners, he was a keen grower of tree fruit and the garden must have looked splendid with blossom in spring time. In the eighteenth century, there were many varieties of fruit trees available, most of which have not survived in general cultivation today. When Goldney laid out a new fruit garden in 1744, he planted 15 varieties of apples, 10 of peaches and 8 each of pears and cherries. These were planted on two sides of a rectangle and on either side of diagonal paths within it; Goldney drew a carefully numbered plan and kept a matching list. Two of the apples he chose – the Golden Pippin and the Nonpareil – were particularly recommended by gardening authors. According to Switzer, peaches and nectarines were much esteemed, and Goldney bought some of the recommended varieties: Noblesse, Montauban and Newington. For the cherries, he chose what were considered the most reliable: May Duke, Carnation, Black and White Heart, and Kentish. As well as buying new trees, Goldney records a great deal of budding and grafting carried out by his own gardeners. They evidently grew their own dwarfing root stock for this, as in August 1744, for instance, the 'Paradise Stocks in the Orchard' were 'budded' with over a dozen varieties of apples. The grafting was not confined to apples, but peaches, nectarines and apricots were also budded on plum stock. It is interesting too that Goldney and his gardener experimented with what are now called 'family' fruit trees, but there are no comments on their success. One example in 1742 was the grafting of 'Jargonel, Green Jennet & Orange Burgamy, on each of the two standard Pear Stocks in the Apple Orchard'. The names alone are a loss to modern gardening.

Vines

Vine-growing seems to have been more widespread in England in the eighteenth century than it is today, and vines were a continuing interest to Goldney. The first reference to a vine growing in his own garden was in February 1738. He was taking cuttings from a 'true white Muscadine Grape', evidently already established on a south-facing wall in his kitchen garden. A year later, in February 1739, although he had just bought Robert Smith's small 'inclosed garden now planted to a vineyard', he planted rows of eight named varieties of vines in his new grotto garden, as well as other cuttings in the kitchen garden. Some of these had come from Philip Miller and the nursery at Chelsea. Goldney, whose own writing was usually clearly legible, complained that one of the labels 'Renraw or Red something' was 'so imperfectly writ as not to be read'. The original vineyard probably became part of what Goldney called the Fort garden, the area south of the bastion, where he planted three more rows of vine cuttings in September 1748. As he also called it the Poultry Garden, the hens must have been scratching about here too. Unfortunately, there are no references to what sort of crop was obtained, but it must have been sufficient to encourage Goldney to persevere, as he added more rows against 'the Sweep-Wall' in the paddock below the Rotunda in 1754. At the same time, more cuttings were planted in the Fountain Garden, near the house, and 'between the Fruit Trees', which would seem to have been less suitable sites than the south-facing slopes below the bastion and rotunda. Of the many varieties available for cultivation, Goldney kept to about a dozen, showing some preference for Muscadine Royal, Burgundy, Frontineack and Black Sweet Water.

Flowers

Some of Goldney's notes show a keen interest in flowers. A theft from his garden in 1749 and the reward he offered suggests that he had some prized things. A notice appeared in a Bristol paper that 'A large collection of Ranunculus's, Anemones, Carnations, and Auriculas' had been stolen on a Sunday night in December, and continued,

> 'Whoever will discover the Person, or Persons, who committed the Robbery, so that he, or they, may be brought to Justice, and Convicted of the same, shall receive Ten Guineas Reward from the said Mr. GOLDNEY.'

There is no evidence of the discovery of the thief or the return of the plants, though the reward must have been tempting. The four flowers mentioned, together with hyacinths, which Goldney also grew, make up five of the 'Seven Capital Shed (or exhibition) Flowers' and it has been suggested that Goldney may have been a 'florist' or connoisseur of certain specialised kinds of flowers. Known as 'florists' flowers', these were grown with meticulous care in attempts to conform to almost unattainable standards of perfection. However, although Goldney grew these and other flowers favoured by florists – hollyhocks, stocks, Sweet Williams and narcissus – there is no evidence that he considered himself a florist, and no references have come to light to show that he entered prize-winning flowers at the 'Annual meetings of Gentlemen Florists', which were reported in the local newspapers.

The most detailed notes of flowers grown by Goldney refer to hyacinths. These seem particularly to have attracted him, though this impression is partly suggested by two chance surviving lists from 1742 and 1750. Double-flowered hyacinths became popular in the eighteenth century and were quite expensive. Goldney's notes record the colours and quality: 'King of Great Britain a fine rose colour'; another, unnamed, is

'A Blew, strip'd with a deeper Blew. This sort is not so very double, but ye different Colours, when it blows strong, are very agreeable'.

Other notes indicate the care he took in planting them:

'Hyacinth of Peru: This should be planted under a Wall in very poor Soil, & not taken up every Year as ye fine Sorts generally are, otherwise (tho twill increase by ye Root very fast) it is not apt to Flower.'

He added a special note:

'Hyacinths, when in Flower, should be pretty much shaded, otherwise the Sun is apt to burn up their Colour'.

Other flowers mentioned by Goldney were mostly grown from seed. He sowed hollyhock seed in a range of colours most years, and larkspur and stocks and a few sunflowers. As with some of his other plants, seeds were often obtained from friends and neighbours, or his gardener Adam, and once his sister Hannah brought him larkspur seed from London. He gathered seed from his own plants, and sometimes kept it too long or not in the right conditions. 1740 was a particularly disappointing year as hollyhock and larkspur seed saved from it 'did not come up' in 1741 or 1743. There are few references to his greenhouse plants, but in the 1760s the Duchess of Northumberland saw

'the Inhabitants of the Green House in very flourishing health ... set out intermix'd with a variety of Flowers. Myrtles grow & flower here very well in the common Ground'.

In the notes about plantings, Goldney occasionally mentions the sources of material. As one would expect, the fruit and other trees generally came from nurseries but, perhaps surprisingly, since there were sources of supply in Bristol, most of those named were in London. Some of them are now famous in gardening history: Philip Miller at Chelsea, Gray and Gordon at Mile End, Peter Collinson at Mill Hill, and Stephen Switzer on Millbank. Goldney bought a large collection of specimen trees from Gray and Gordon's nursery in 1755 to plant along his new southern boundary; these included several pines, such as Lord Weymouth's [*Pinus strobus*], Frankincense [*Pinus taeda*] and Balm of Gilead [*Abies balsamea*], and two Cedars of Lebanon [*Cedrus libani*]. At the same time he bought nearly a dozen varieties of what he called haws or thorns [*Crataegus*] to plant at the eastern end of the paddock. A local nurseryman who supplied plum trees was William Cheney of Stokes Croft. Cuttings, seeds and what Goldney called 'roots', usually bulbs, came from neighbours like Robert Smith, other Clifton residents and friends, and a cousin who had a large house and estate at Luckenham, Wiltshire.

Gardeners

The ideas for the planning and construction of the garden and even some of the work in the grotto seem to have been Thomas Goldney's own, but for the planting, cultivation and maintenance he depended on his gardeners. He was fortunate in the first appointment he made in 1732. Adam Sixsmith, the man he chose to take charge of the original garden, remained with Goldney until his master's death in 1768. When Sixsmith was first appointed at a salary of £12 a year, there were just over two acres to attend to, but 25 years later, this had increased to about 16 acres, including the extra kitchen garden, the paddocks and Hill Close; for the care of this larger estate and various other duties he was paid £15 a year. This compared quite well with the wages some head gardeners of much larger estates were paid. There is no mention of rent free or other accommodation until 1766 when he was given a life interest in a cottage Goldney had just bought. It needed repair, but was worth £6 a year in rent. Sixsmith did not need it for his own occupation as from 1758 he had owned the lease of a house conveniently situated down the hill on Woodwell Lane [now Jacobs Wells Road]. The names mentioned in the lease suggest that he was unmarried with no children of his own. From the mid 1740s to about 1760 there was also an assistant gardener, Ralph Seddon, and later Sixsmith's nephew, also Adam, was employed. Adam Sixsmith the elder died in January 1775 and was buried in the churchyard at Clifton across the green from Goldney house.

The names of the two gardeners occur frequently in Goldney's Garden Book; Adam Sixsmith is almost always mentioned by his first name, which perhaps suggests a degree of friendship between master and servant. The legacy of £50 left to him in Thomas Goldney's will was the largest amount bequeathed to any of the servants. Both gardeners were literate and their signatures occur as witnesses to some of the estate deeds. As well as notes about the budding and grafting carried out by his gardeners, Goldney also recorded occasions when the men worked particularly zealously: in May 1738 Adam

> 'mowed the Long Walk and Greenhouse Walk by nine a clock in the morning but then he rose between 3 and 4.'

In June the same year, he

'shear'd all ye Greens in ye Long Walk (ye high hollys included) in 2 days & ¹/₂, & finish'd ye Box Edgings in Ditto Walk in about 2 days & ¹/₄ but then he work'd these days till past Eight in ye Evening beginning early in ye Morning'.

Twenty-five years later, the Duchess was impressed by this 'row of variegated Standard Hollys of an incredible height'. In late May 1746, the two gardeners 'Mow'd the 2 long Walks, the Wilderness, & all ye other Walks in ye lower Garden, in one Morning before X, Rose at III.'

These were no mean feats without the aid of modern tools, such as lawn-mowers and powered hedge-trimmers. However, garden rollers have not changed much in design; the ones used in Goldney garden were cast iron, supplied from Coalbrookdale, and the largest weighed over seven hundredweight. One wonders whether it was preparation for a special occasion or the advent of an honoured visitor that prompted these unusual efforts. That Goldney recorded them suggested he appreciated his gardeners' activities and their devotion to their work.

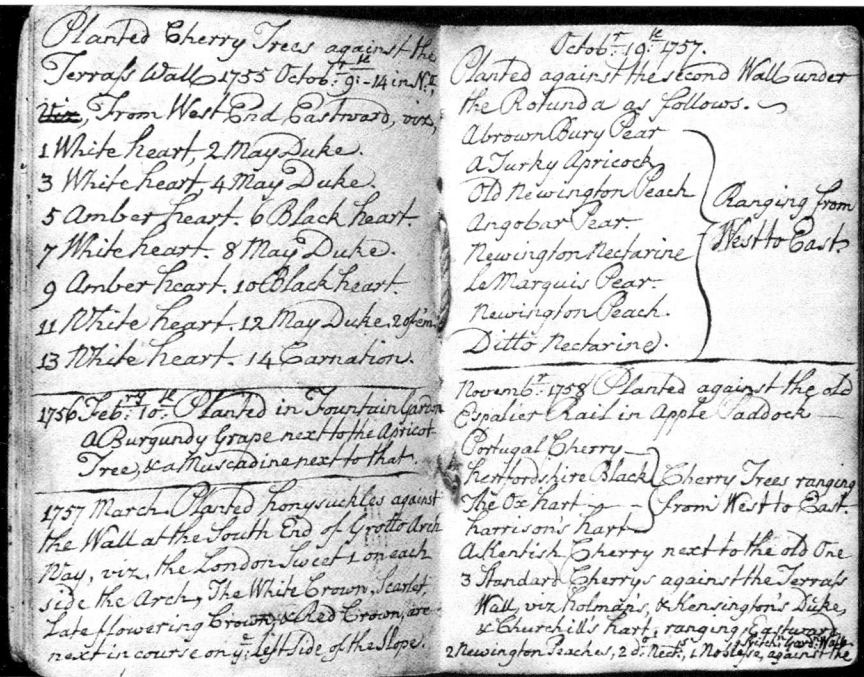

Pages from Thomas Goldney's Garden Book.

University of Bristol

Layout and design

The Duchess of Northumberland thought the garden was 'rather formal but not ugly'. She might well have thought the same of the original design. At no time in the eighteenth century was Goldney garden in the fashion. The map of 1746, though obviously not accurate in every detail, suggests that the nucleus of the garden to the south of the house was divided by walks into triangular 'quarters'. The only other source of evidence for the layout is in the notes Goldney made in the Garden Book that he had begun to keep in the autumn of 1736. He mentions various areas, for instance: 'asparagrass', 'cowcumber', and mould quarters, elm, holly and yew walks, statues, and the fountain garden, but it is not easy to identify the positions of any of these. Goldney of course had no need to include explanatory details, as his notes were just for his own use. The entries became very infrequent in the 1750s, when he was much occupied with the expansion of the iron works at Coalbrookdale, and stopped altogether at the crucial time in 1758 although there was still space in the note book. The pattern of the garden must have changed gradually at first until the major re-organisation of the original main garden took place in the late 1750s and early 1760s, with the construction of the canal, and the re-positioning of the greenhouse or orangery from the west walk to the commanding position in relation to the canal.

For the site of the garden the final design is not inappropriate nor out of proportion to the area. Goldney envisaged the formal closely planted central section with plenty of green space on the southern and western boundaries; sadly, much of the latter has been lost to development in the second half of the nineteenth century, and even more has gone in the later twentieth century with buildings encroaching on the bastion and the west walk. This has seriously affected what was obviously a major attraction and a significant feature of the garden in the eighteenth and nineteenth centuries: the prospect. Thomas Goldney had bought surrounding land so that the heart of his garden should not be overlooked, but he had also contrived splendid viewing points to look outward, particularly over the slopes of Clifton Wood to the river and beyond to the Somerset countryside. Visitors like Mrs Delany enthused about the prospect:

'hedge rows, clumps of trees, and woods all happily placed; the city of Bristol; the windings of the river, and sailing boats and barges; the stupendous rocks,... from a terrace in Mr. Golding's garden we saw everything in the utmost perfection.'

The Duchess of Northumberland was equally impressed: 'ye View is extensive & very fine over the Downs the Wells the Fields Dundry Tower ....

&c'. The very minor poet, William Heard, devoted several dozen lines of *A Sentimental Journey,* published in 1778, to the splendours of Clifton and to Mr Goldney's garden and grotto and the views from the terrace.

Focal points for views within the garden still exist: the tower, the rotunda and the statue of Hercules at the end of the yew walk above the grotto entrance, but there were more walks with statues in Goldney's time. The statues seem to have been a miscellaneous collection, some possibly remaining from the ownership of Lord Folliot; nor were they as appropriately placed as Batty Langley had suggested in *New Principles of Gardening* published in 1723. Ceres, for instance, could be in woods and groves, but at Goldney she was in the front courtyard, accompanied by Bacchus, who might have been better placed among the vines; a Roman soldier would certainly have produced a surprise in the Holly Walk. According to the Duchess, one of the walks looked

> 'to a Wall Mr Gouldney has had ... painted as a large Arch of a Bridge thro wch you appear to see the Sea an Island & a Fort so well done as almost to deceive you'.

This was another example of Goldney's idiosyncratic taste, though he may have been following an idea, also suggested by Batty Langley years before, that paintings of ancient ruins could be placed at the ends of 'walks as must terminate within the Garden'. In the 1770s, Gabriel Goldney paid the Bristol scene painter, Michael Edkins, five and a half guineas for 'Cleaning Stopping Varnishing and entirely new Painting a large Scene which terminates a Walk in the Garden'. So another piece of Goldney's fantasy was evidently appreciated and maintained by others.

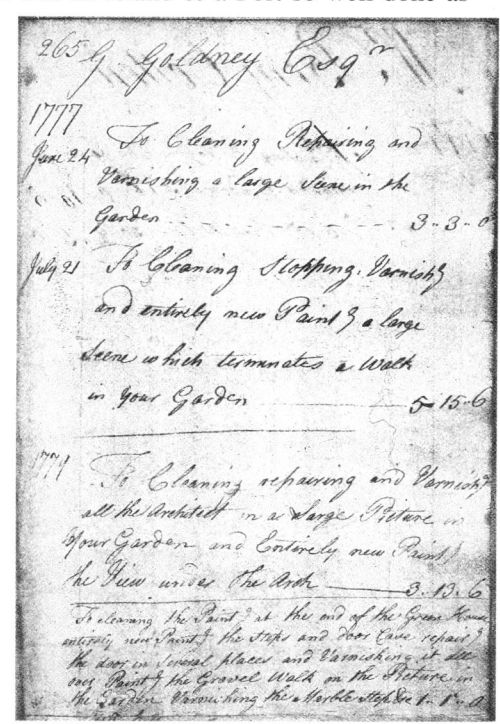

Local Studies Library, Bristol Reference Library

Account book of Michael Edkins.

Visitors and Fame

Visiting gardens was popular with travellers in the eighteenth century and visitors were often taken round by the head gardener, who was then very likely given 'vails' or tips as well as the satisfaction of hearing praise for a well-maintained garden. Many more people must have come to Goldney than have left accounts in letters or journals. The earliest visitor we know of was John Kelsall who belonged to the Quaker circle and was invited with other Friends for social occasions at Goldney during his stay in Bristol. The Revd Alexander Catcott who visited in 1749 belonged to a Bristol family and was much interested in geology and curiosities. He was also evidently interested in gardening as he had given Goldney '2 early Hyacinth Roots' and 'two roots of Crown Imperial' in the summer of 1747. His account records the progress made in the construction of the grotto and Goldney told him about his plans for the cascade and the basin or pool at its foot.

Mrs Delany, who had friends at court and among the aristocracy, had obviously heard of the garden and especially the grotto before she came to Bristol in 1756. She visited the garden with some Clifton friends 'by appointment'. In a letter to her sister, she wrote,

> 'I will not say a very elegant fancy might not have made the whole better, but it is by much the finest thing of the kind I ever saw; though I could not but grudge at the shells sacrificed there, and exposed to the ruin of damp and time, that would have preserved their beauty for ages in a cabinet! The master is reckoned a great humourist and a niggard, but I was so fortunate as to take his fancy, and he gave me two or three pretty specimens of coral, and said I should have what I pleased.'

In spite of getting Goldney's name wrong, she was treated more generously by him than by the Revd Alexander Catcott, whose collection she had admired the same morning. She probably put in a request on behalf of her friend the Duchess of Portland, as some time later Goldney sent the Duchess a quantity of Bristol diamonds, lead ore and spar for her grotto at Bulstrode. Mrs Andrew Grote, a London banker's wife, was brought by one of Goldney's fellow bank directors in 1762 especially to see the grotto which she greatly admired, and she was also impressed because 'Mr Goldney made it all himself'. The Duchess of Northumberland, visiting at about the same period, evidently found the house and particularly the garden very interesting, as she left a much longer description of Goldney than of several of the more extensive gardens in the district that she visited the same season. The Austrian Count Karl von Zinzendorf came in September 1768 and he too was favourably impressed with all that he saw. His description of Goldney is among his accounts of Stoke Park, Kingsweston, Stourhead and other famous gardens elsewhere in Britain, which suggests how well Goldney ranked among them.

The agriculturist Arthur Young visited Goldney in 1766 or 1767 while gathering information for his book *A Tour of the Southern Counties,* but he was rather grudging in his comments, perhaps affected by the difficulty he claimed to have had in getting in to see the garden. He thought the grotto was 'curious in materials and taste', though he admired the shells, fossils, corals and spar, etc., which were 'all in greater plenty, and better of their sort, than in any grotto I have seen'. He commented unfavourably on the plain skylights, wishing for some more subtle form of lighting. Young was one of the last visitors in Thomas Goldney's lifetime, but others came in following years while the garden was owned first by his brother Gabriel and then by their sister Ann till almost the end of the century. At this time, entry to the garden seems to have been by ticket. When the American, Samuel Curwen, who left such a detailed and useful description, came on his first visit in 1776, a friend had procured tickets for a small group. Numbers of visitors to the Hotwell probably found an excursion to the garden and grotto a welcome diversion. After an enthusiastic description of Clifton and its attractions in his *Bristol Directory* of 1793, William Matthews included a paragraph on Mrs Goldney's house, 'celebrated for a curious grotto', and suggested that readers should see it for themselves as 'access is granted to proper persons'. John Wesley visited in September 1788, and was particularly impressed by the long terrace walk. He admired the grotto and, after commenting on the years Mr Goldney had spent in collecting and placing the 'variety of shells and glittering fossils', concluded ruefully 'and he has left it all'.

Goldney garden, and particularly the grotto, was obviously well-known long before it was complete and was much visited in the eighteenth century. During the nineteenth century the house became a more private family home again: for sixty years for the Goldney cousins from Chippenham and their descendants, and then for another sixty years for Lewis Fry and his family into the beginning of the twentieth century. Mr and Mrs Ellison Eberle, who bought the property in the 1930s, took a great interest in its history and that of the two Goldneys, father and son, who had built the house and created the garden. As a result of their interest, two illustrated articles appeared in *Country Life,* and later Pevsner filled a page in *Buildings of England: North Somerset and Bristol,* describing the 'enviable gardens' and 'the most enchanting ornament ... the Grotto'. More recently, the grotto has been listed on the English Heritage Register as Grade I and the other garden features as Grade II*. Since 1969, when the house became the nucleus of a new hall of residence for students from the University of Bristol and flats for students were built on part of Hill Close, many thousands of visitors have come on days when the gardens are open to the public or for special occasions to enjoy and admire them. Praised by the poet as 'a minor Stow on Clifton's crown', Thomas Goldney's unique creation has not only given pleasure to thousands but has also acquired an important place in garden history.

Acknowledgements

This account of Goldney garden during the three centuries of its existence is based on the items of contemporary evidence that have survived: estate deeds, a garden notebook, a memorandum book, a business ledger and visitors' accounts. Thanks are due to the staff of the record offices, museums and libraries, particularly Mr Nick Lee of the University of Bristol Library, who have made documents and illustrations available. I am grateful to many friends who, over the years, have discussed aspects of the garden and provided items of information and who, more recently, have commented on the illustrations and the text. I am especially grateful to David Lambert for additional visitors' accounts and his comments, and to Dr John Harvey for sharing his wide knowledge and identifying the trees and plants mentioned in the Garden Book. Any errors of fact and interpretation are my responsibility. The Avon Gardens Trust has generously supplied the funds for publication to mark the tercentenary in July 1996 of the birth of Thomas Goldney III and Mr David Corrigan of Burleigh Press has patiently provided expertise with the text and design.

30